GOBLIN LAWN

Also by Peter Bennet

First Impressions (Mandeville)
Sky-riding (Peterloo)
The Border Hunt (Jackson's Arm)
A Clee Sequence (Lincolnshire and Humberside Arts)
All the Real (Flambard)
The Long Pack (Flambard)
Ha-Ha (Smith/Doorstop)
Noctua (Shoestring)

GOBLIN LAWN

New and Selected Poems

Peter Bennet

FlambardPress

First published in Great Britain in 2005 by Flambard Press
Stable Cottage, East Fourstones, Hexham NE47 5DX

Typeset by BookType
Front-cover image: 'Boy Bird's Nesting', a woodcut by Eric Ravilious,
reproduced by kind permission of Merivale Editions
© Estate of Eric Ravilious 2005; all rights reserved, DACS
Cover design by Gainford Design Associates
Printed in Great Britain by Cromwell Press, Trowbridge, Wiltshire

A CIP catalogue record for this book
is available from the British Library.

ISBN 1 873226 77 2

Flambard Press wishes to thank Arts Council England
for its financial support.

website: www.flambardpress.co.uk

Flambard Press is a member of Inpress
and Independent Northern Publishers.

CONTENTS

To the one-eye hills and the mordant hour

Author's Note

The poems in this collection were completed between 1999 and 2004, though parts of 'The Long Pack' and 'Jigger Nods' were written earlier. Acknowledgements and thanks are due to Flambard Press, Shoestring Press, and Smith/Doorstop Books. 'Ogress' first appeared in *The Rialto*. 'The Pear Tree' was included in *The Way You Say the World: a Celebration for Anne Stevenson*.

Peter Bennet gratefully acknowledges receipt of a Northern Writers' Award from New Writing North and Arts Council England.

from HA-HA

HA-HA

Let me affirm that what I have not done
remains a plant so valueless
that I have never learned its shape or name.

It thrives, a clump of uncommitted spirit,
between me and the *saut-de-loup*, or ha-ha.

It was in Paris, or on the Riviera,
entre deux guerres, for sure, that someone
quite unknown to me, but close,
had picked a bunch, and tied it with a ribbon,
to throw into a grave I will not enter.

IF NOT

for Sean O'Brien

When you were young, you saw the future,
but elegantly turned your back
in topaz light, re-entering
the schloss above its village of retainers,
among your vivid hills and tinkling pastures.

The refugees have lit a fire,
and sit cross-legged on a traffic island.

In your bedroom, in that painting
of the blond boys diving
into a forest pool with turquoise water,
I recognise the naked policeman
posing like a question-mark.

Your flesh still fits you like a glove.

Old nature-worshipper, I know how much
it used to cost you to adore
the sun in luxury:
can you propitiate the thunder
that starts to sound like oil drums bumping
up the steps of your hotel?

Be quiet, or I'll break your bones.

Teach me about art, and truth and beauty,
and I'll fix papers, local currency.

Teach me how to be like you, if not
you'll end up eating your own shoes.

THE BROAD WALK

Here is the place to promenade,
shopgirls and ladies,
while opening your hearts in conversation
beneath an avenue of limes.

A clergyman is pacing out his sermon.

Modest deshabille is now permitted,
but young men are importunate, and apt
to take advantage
of those who stray beyond convention.

An artist sets his easel in the shade.

Ruin will also try to make an assignation:
you can't mistake
her red, insistant, gin-blotched features.

A novelist removes his towering hat,
extracting a small notebook from it.

Oh dear, the mist is lifting from the fields
and from the river,
revealing the dissolving face
of she we last saw quite disordered,
for whom the broad walk offered no protection.

CLARET

If this emergency were not so pressing,
we might have rested here another evening
and talked of any foolishness:
the wine stains on this map,
the sound that time makes falling through my mind.

You're as young as I was once: I know you
as if I looked out from your shaving-mirror.

I saw you smile to see the squadron wheel
through smoke, sunlight instantly on sabre blades,
for all the world, in all that slaughter,
like shoals of pretty silver fish.

You're right, there is a kind of beauty in it.

I read somewhere that when a man
feels most oppressed,
his spirit is achieving freedom.

This morning, did you notice, as our column
passed the burning church,
how that old woman spat upon my shadow,
and how she held her thumb and fingers?

I have decided.

Please pay close attention:
that is the place where we shall take positions,
yes there, where claret stained it red.

THE FOUNTAIN

Nothing happens here, except
the village keeps on climbing up the valley.

Still these sky-high draughty windows
with slagheaps peering in all afternoon
and only furniture for company.

The days seem shorter, even so.

Last night I took the box from underneath the bed
and burnt your birth certificate,
your photographs, and all those inky letters
you used to write to me from school.

It's getting chilly.

Come on, come on, my father used to say,
leave the stilton and the biscuits,
let's go and see the fountain in the snow,
the water and the dry snow falling,
and hear that water-babble fill the dark.

DEEP HEDGES

You are the saddest part of that idea
of art which loves a sweet, immobile odour,
damp flagstones and a door that sticks,
unwashed dishes, mouse tracks in the larder,
and womanless arrival of old age.

Your work has been a kite flown in a mist,
the cutting string tugged sharply taut
by something high, something invisible.

I'll keep this short and try to keep it simple.

Each of your slogging compositions
seemed a new beginning, but your symbols,
traditional though finely wrought, refuse
to spring to life and cause a transformation.

The road itself twists to avoid your house
and hurries, in an English fashion,
between deep hedges laden with excuses
down towards the pub and sunlit steeple.

THE ENGINE

Here are my shells, arranged on their green saucer,
my window and its view: a complex thicket.

Beyond that is a sloping reach of earth
like tarnished copper, patterned by the plough.

For a long time I had nightmares in this room.

Now I know how best to start the engine
that overrides my false, mistaken thinking.

This landscape folds upon itself, as I do,
now that the wind blows from the west all day
and will not cause discomfort or reflection.

Look over there, against the sun.

I remember, when I walked into that copse,
how intimacy conquered distance
and detail woke in me: a bullfinch flock
were jewels among beech leaves, flickering
then rising in a cloud to vanish
like murders I commit while I'm asleep.

GENEALOGY

Since yesterday, it seems, the maps have changed,
the church clock cannot tell the time,
the names you want have faded from the microfiche,
and from the xeroxed parish registers.

The village is beneath the town,
the town is underneath the city.

Just think, the letter from your ancestor
that would have made the whole thing clear, the task
so simple, put aside and never finished,
because a moth got in the inkwell.

Call it a day.

You'd starve, in any case, if you went back,
the past contains no sustenance,
the birthday cakes are grey with dust,
the orchards there grow only apple cores.

Look now, at the changing creature
here in the hedge, made out of leaves: its tiny
limbs reach out for recognition.

Its colour goes so suddenly from green
to splintering silver: can you see it, dare you touch?

WAKEFUL

The finger-holds are undercut, and shallow.

The escritoire is mainly empty:
unimportant correspondence,
a file of cuttings from the local paper,
some company prospectuses.

One drawer is locked, although it slides,
perhaps a quarter-inch, its lock being worn,
and from it comes a scent of roses.

Nothing has been tampered with.

All's well, within the heart of England's dream,
as long as men like us are wakeful.

Fling back the casements and breathe in the air.

The croquet lawn is fringed by elms
untouched by age, its perfect turf
accepts the tribute of the evening sun.

The London train has been and gone.

Beyond that glimpse of farmhouse roofs
and patient cattle, one approaches,
whose face is pretty but whose mien is furtive,
whose reticule conceals a loaded gun.

CONTENT

Time ripens in abundance, hanging
unplucked while he examines the horizon,
or shies selected stones at driftwood.

Since exile here, he understands
he is a figment of his own imagination.

His mind is now becoming like the ocean
on which he sometimes fancies glimpses
of distant ships, or makes some speck
a swimmer's head, small waves
the rocking angles of a swimmer's arms.

Solitude, and lack of tools or toys
do not constrain him: he can visit
all his wishes, walk or run, repeat his journeys,
act on impulses or cancel them,
and name things or decide to leave them nameless.

He is content to be passed over
by infrequent clouds, and birds
with gaudy wings and human voices.

He disregards the long-haul airliner
whose dreamy passengers can hardly see
his island, let alone
the threats to trespassers he has inscribed
in foliage across the broadest beach.

FILMING THE LIFE

Your sisters have agreed to drag their skirts
across the fields where trees are shrugging
coldly, as it is October,
towards the lane with hedges, and the gate
where gravel leads to wider gravel
and damp-stains on the quoining of the manse.

We have the Bible on the hallstand,
adjacent to the wet umbrella,
and cabbage in a kitchen full of women.

The draughts at ankle-height across the flagstones
come from the hills on which your father wanders,
prising sermons from the mist and boulders.

Your role now is to find an upstairs room
and be the ghost-child at a pointed window,
offering his breath to glass
in order to inscribe it, and then seeing
a darker world on which his name is weeping.

You are too sickly to grow old,
and will not live to see your pamphlets smoulder
in every bookshop of the revolution.

UNAIDED

Think how the kestrel reappeared
above the rookery
as many times as crows chased him away,
and how the snow-gusts in the orchard
lacked conviction, and the air at noon
was warm, and had the taste of flowers.

Turn on your pillow, sleepy head.

Think of the candlesticks of Bishop Bernard
you carved, unaided, through the winter,
with naked sinners climbing vegetation
towards the light, the candle-flame
that animates their quick, entangled limbs.

Tomorrow you will work with zeal,
despite new evidence
to prove the malice of your fellow masons.

Before the act, you have forgiven
the poor apprentice who will steal your savings
during the hour of meditation.

SPALPEEN

Time's up for you inside my myth,
so shout at every turning of the tune,
and clap your hands
to have this moment for your pleasure.

Fact steps forward to reveal you,
clean-shaven, and of medium height,
like every spalpeen in the land.

Outside, trams flash and clang
through Celtic twilight, and the rain
that slicks the courtyard of the School of Art
shines the stone limbs of Cuchulain,
the lord of skirmish and unlucky frolic.

You gave me nothing but permission.

I was your shadow, and my dumb attention
a story harped on long ago
which made for grief, just as the love
of my fair rival, Kathleen of the duffel coat,
led towards the lake of weeping.

CHA-CHA-CHA

Evening achieves a winter definition:
the gravel stark between metallic laurels,
and your french window lit too brightly
to countenance my pale reflection.

I formed you out of fog and petrol fumes
outside the walls of colleges
where gargoyles sneer above shut doors,
and now I'm here, according to my custom,
to tap discreetly on your glass and enter
for sherry, and rich conversation
among your art and incunabula.

Although your back is turned towards me,
I see your well-trimmed head is as I shaped it,
together with the light, informal jacket
above dark trousers with an iron crease.

There should not be a gramophone, however,
unless for Mozart, and it puzzles me
to hear one faintly honking cha-cha-cha.

You are my creature and my ideal tutor,
the man to help me get my thinking baked
and spiced with wit and erudition,
the chum I can rely on always
urbanely to correct my sentences.

But please remember that your cosy room
will freeze if ever I should wish it,
and you will shrivel and no longer be.

Forgive me if I seem at all ungrateful.

It's who you're talking to that makes me peevish,
her sleek legs angled to the hearth
from that deep armchair sacred to philosophy,
and how, when she in turn begins to speak,
her head uptilts, a smoke-ring hanging,
to notice me, then mock me with a wink.

DOWN UNDER

with thanks to Terence Blacker

Of course I know the spit, the river's elbow
at which we picnic, where the sun
shines kindly through the plane trees and the elms.

Each night, before I sleep, I swim
and let the swollen water there
carry me downstream in safety.

The essence of the place, each time I visit,
remains the same as when I, when I:
but then, forgetting falls on what won't fit,
and things transmogrify, when called to mind,
to match the bright, receding pattern.

There go the sulphur-crested cockatoos,
the sacred ibis pecking dapples
beside us on the warm grass as you, as you.

What makes the contours of the land vibrate
to slough the skin of years, again revealing
the almost-hidden paradise,
is only that we meet here when we, when we
add to the best time of our bodies
the music of geography,
like lovers in a Springsteen song.

We are outrageously, absurdly blessed,
but disagree about the other music
that echoes from the farther bank more loudly
now that the paddle steamer is approaching
that carries on its deck our wedding party.

T.E. LAWRENCE NEAR CLOUDS HILL

The place is lonely, very bare,
and furnished with three chairs, a bed,
one hundred books, a gramophone.

See how, in these last moments, I descend
the gravel slopes, where clumps of grass
become more frequent, and the impure sand
is seamed with dry and brittle clay.

I did not sleep there, but came out
each evening, if I could, to write and dream.

Here are remembered traces of old floods
through which my camel sinks in dust
thickened like soup by sunlight held
where dead air of the wadi lies a-dazzle.

Wild mares would not persuade me elsewhere now.

The hills come closer, and the valley fills
with brushwood, sideways from the mounds,
bone-dry, and reaching in entanglements
to pluck the streamers of my saddle-bags.

This life has been a rare adventure.

I shall draw in my cloak and bend my head
to guard my eyes above the handlebars
and crash through like a storm through reeds.

REMITTANCE

The breathing of an ocean stirs the leaves
and flips my collar up to kiss my neck,
and strokes my spine, according to the tune
rigging hums along the jetty.

I remain, Sir, your imprisoned butterfly,
that has no conscience, and the house
I share, with my unseemly lover,
has lilac shutters among daffodils.

Sulphur-tinted, and the shape of flame,
I fit your shadow perfectly
beside the table where you squint
at stark white napery,
and make a glass squeak with your moistened finger.

You will remember what I know. Hereafter,
my freedom must be paid for with your money.

NOTHING WORSE

You do not know this, but your standard lamp
has been sawn through, a foot below the shade.

Meanwhile, the river swells and flows on grass,
a pasture swallowing its fences, green
contending, overcoming green, until
the stink and rush, from this high viaduct,
suggests that nothing human will outlast
leeching eels, and rain, and livid sky.

Come back with me into your sitting-room.

The party you walked out on has concluded
in nothing worse than friendly sabotage.

DEAREST

Today it feels like thunder, getting hot
but darker on this fever field
of khaki tents beneath the khaki mountain.

I like to picture you behind your window,
missing me as day shuts down, and English
shrubbery seems closer, soaking up the light.

The chaps here are a decent crowd.

The last big capture took a lot, and now
our problem is with transport, all we had
we sent ahead and sit here stinking
of river mud and refuse pits,
tarpaulins, and forage, and dead horses.

Even insects are asleep, the gawping daisies
are quite immobile in the grass, and poppies,
which are the colour of our separation.

It seems that only words are on the move.

Somewhere there's a mouth-organ, and rag-time,
and someone drumming on a plate, and then
its *you*, and something you were singing, clipping
rose stems for the bowl before the mirror.

Do you remember? Will you write it down?

Now the sky has slipped a little,
hanging low, and at an angle.

Next winter when I'm home, and cold and cozy,
we shall stack and burn our kisses.

TITHONUS AT KIELDER

Since death avoids you, every longed-for morning
hurts worse than death, and evenings turn
from grey to purple without hope.

Cheer up, old grasshopper, at least
you had the guts to claim the dawn
before the hours indignant worked their wills.

The woods decay and fall, so fell
and plant again, and celebrate your days
as if they danced like sunlit leaves
caught in the backstream of a timber waggon
returning on its silver wheels.

THE LONG PACK

I tremble to tell you! We are all gone, for it is a living pack.

James Hogg

Northumberland is a rough county.

Sir Nikolaus Pevsner

I

Darkness is my second mother,
the pack a double blindness, in whose caul
I must not move,
but grip my butcher's knife, my silver whistle,
and wait till silence matches dark,
to cut free like a savage child.

I am about my act, my strange acte,
my worke, my strange work.

II

Now Bellingham is briefly hers.

The oiled gate
is quiet as a book to open.

Inside, the yew tree is a flame's
dark opposite,
smudged upon the inner eye,
it struggles upward, angled to its stem,
and cannot leave the ground.

My stone's a lid on grass,
but mind is calling me to mind, as if
I might be here awake and answering
bones above the layered bones.

The iron latch-tail chills,
and clings to moisture on her palm.

I'm seeing what I don't remember,
and so are you, imagining my fear,
and sacking chafing at my face.

I breathe stale merchandise,
and, as a lantern flares through cloth,
embrace a tremor in the air.

Whosoever hears of it,
both his ears shall tingle.

III

At sunset, Midas fished the Tyne,
or else the gentry of Northumberland
are melting all their riches down.

Gold slides past kingcups to the sea,
but here, where common boulders sit,
colours are of coal and lead.

My father stumbles from the flow:
his hands are empty, but his head
has feasted on philosophy.

That man he countless times heard preach
against the rule and stink of priests maintained,
one Lord's day sixty years ago,
he met God walking in an open field,
to his eyes seeming strange,
a man deformed, clad in patched clouts.

God looked wishly on him, and he pittied God.

The Tyne would bubble like a sore
if it absorbed
the rage my father steeps in it.

Our supper slips to deeper water.

IV

Time rattles in the ewe's throat.

Mist blots up stories from the fell,
muffles moorland industry, conceals
herd and soldier, park and steading,
tumulus and battlestone,
the horse that bolted with the bride,
lots drawn, stratagems forgotten.

The dead do not know who they are
until they are remembered.

V

A fly strums glass,
and bumps the distances your window holds.

Blue hills, remembering to be
Roxburghshire, across the Border,
stand for all that's torn away,
like Houxty Wood:
the nymphs lamenting for their dear resort.

The fly is stitching
shreds of history to hills,
and patching nearer times with fields.

The past lies in the sun beyond the pane.

Art poor? Yea, very poor, said He.

VI

At Warden, where the two Tynes meet
behind my father's empty hands,
I see the solemn water break
into a curve of countless brilliants
across my memory, as rich and starry
as Colonel Ridley's chandeliers,
and one great salmon in their midst
stand upon its tail for ever.

This is a true story, most true in the history.

The fish is one of diverse signs
that comfort me
in this concealment where I am
still visible,
if you will please imagine it.

The plague of God is in your purses,
did you not see my hand stretched out?

VII

She thumbs an apple in her pocket
and somewhere thunder scrapes a drum.

The fieldgate jigs,
its wreckage flouncing baler-twine.

Sunlight on a shattered gable
hints at past prosperity:
The Orchard on its tidy portion.

Drystone dikes beside the path
rise again among the nettles,
and deeply fumbling ruts reveal
the old highroad across the Rede,
broad enough for carts to pass, or haul
harvest towers, two abreast.

Tyme tryeth Troth.

Her apple pleases
a roan mare by the broken barn.

VIII

The Jacobite rose-bush
strikes your wall with small, white blossoms.

Fallen petals sign the ground:
Derwentwater, Forster, Mad Jack Hall.

Northumberland is Arcady.

The paperback you've pushed aside
has Radcliffe an Initiate,
the rose a mystery
bred by the Prieuré de Sion.

IX

It is meat and drink to an Angel
to swear a full-mouthed oath.

The deeds and discourse
of that great engine of disorder, Richard Last,
so pressed my father's waxy spirit
that two-score years of witnessing
and sundry buffetings we all and each endured
have not ground smooth their stamp.

Neither the death of Mr Last
in this world, or the dissolution
of his lewd company,
nor yet the ruination of our farm,
the self-same Orchard, could abate
his whistling multifarious fancies.

My deer ones consider,
here is no lodging, no safe habitation.

X

Lord of the wood was my game once:
Rob o' Risingham and Robin Hood,
the king within the oak in summer time.

The Oak-Leaves me embroyder all,
between them Caterpillars crawl
and Ivy, with familiar trails,
me licks, and clasps, and curls, and hales.

A boy's face, smiling among leaves,
tells me I shall live again.

XI

To be alone is always new.

Outside your window, past the rosebush
and the garden, moorland pasture
steeps its skirts in the arriving night.

Booze turns the landscape into art.

Cloudscapes you have watched since noon
are smouldering and charged with thunder,
while fells regroup as gloomy leas
and boskage: school of Claude Lorraine.

Pools and streams snag threads of light
in jagged valleys and defiles.

Above Greenrigg, a crabwise track
climbs gothic heights
towards a crumbling tower of cumulus.

You see a well, which sad trees overhang,
and flame and woodsmoke by a ruined arch,
or in some bouldered clearing,
and, always there, the same two countrymen
in ragged costume of their age.

The elder stoops to coax the fire, the younger
leans forward on his staff. Sometimes
they picturesquely fish a stream
or crouch as if in hope beside the path.

I am found of those that sought me not.

XII

The Karrimor rucksack biffs the ground
and stillness
steps into the air behind her.

The weight she cannot feel but as a pulse
of unexpected modesty
is only our attention resting
beside her in the holly garden.

Tasselled nettles, ivy with its frog-shaped leaves,
are seeking what they most resemble.

Solvitur ambulando.

Drops of water on the leaves of holly
remind her of fragility:
but all at once the hopelessness
her erstwhile husband, Dr Pordage, calls
'a little seasonal depression'
seems light enough for all such surfaces.

In Jesmond, her thesis on the pastoral mode
awaits completion
in black bin-liners by a makeshift desk.

XIII

Come, let us goe, while we are in our prime,
and take the harmless follie of the time.

Our one flesh, Marjorie,
that was a chandler's wife at Hexham,
had pissed my mother's bed in drink
the night they put me to her.

Last and my father preached extempore
and my flesh rose.

What God has cleansed, call thou not uncleane.

XIV

With little interruption by its islands,
the Indian Ocean
vastly folds and smooths its rigs.

Beach fires of the heathen raise
a level smoke veil
that separates the sea-flats and the bastion,
and laden barges from the masts at anchor.

Within a cannon-shot of Fort St George,
a resting ox looks up at whip crack,
another, and a distant cry,
to witness English law enacted.

My father ploughed with oxen still
the cloud-swabbed slope below The Orchard,
before the sheep came everywhere
and Richard Last began to preach and print
the blood that crieth in the ears.

His rigs are there for evening sun to notice
as if a grassy main had clenched
the farm, and that become a wrecked stone ship,
its cargo sunk into the moor.

The sea forgives the keel its furrow.

XV

The treasure came to port at London,
and then aboard a collier vessel
pertaining to Sir William Blackett, Baronet,
and then by cart from Newcastle.

That, I myself was witness to.

There is a little sparke lies under
thine honour, pomp and riches,
which shall consume, as it is written.

XVI

Howl, howl, ye nobles, howl honourable,
for the miseries that come upon you.

Is your face towards the light?

Even a tendril of the rose-bush
the night wind stirs against your wall
will leave a groove an axe might cut.

Together, remember, we have cauled
the youth I was
in darkness and a pedlar's pack,
while time in Lee Hall kitchen ticks
three hundred years
against the measure of my heart.

Are you in trembling of a rich man's clock?

Consider the spine of one great tree,
its branches lopped, its saw cut vertebrae
tumbled into English grass.

For our parts, wee'l have all things common,
wee'l break our bread from house to house.

XVII

The housemaid's whisper frightens me.

Come, our wanderer is a shepherdess
whose thoughts are grazing
in sunlit parkland, where a fine grey house
stands back politely,
paid-for out of coal and lead.

Passion plucks no berries
from the myrtle and ivy
nor calls upon Arethuse and Mincius,
nor tells of rough satyrs, and fauns
with cloven heel . . .

Trim nails against the texture of her page
prevent a breeze from turning it.

Is this thy love, thy dove, thy fair one?

Consoling emblems slip my mind,
and she has closed her eyes to see them:
the salmon in its pelt of light,
the treasure cart,
and then the very last I saw
before tarred cloth enveloped me,
a white bull, motionless
against the gathered and substantial dark
of Houxty Wood,
and the moon and stars in ecstasy.

I must not move.

XVIII

Claude's pictures fade, and leave your window
locked darkly on Northumberland.

Chesterhope's a muddy doormat:
you are a poem-spider trod thereon.

What have we then? A revelation?
Or normal untruth soaking bones
of whinstone in a bleating mist?

There's more to pastoral than meets the eye.

XIX

My honeymoon left me a widower:
a mourner at an empty grave, moreover,
and still the priest to pay.

As high of heart as she would ride of old,
Helen, who that wild day in death's despite
escaped the durance of the churchyard mould.

Thus I have also known despair.

XX

How will you meet her, by the way?

She reads the papers. You could try,
sincere male wishes (ho ho)
for friendship and outings (ha ha).

No no.

Be wise now therefore. O ye Rulers
be instructed. Give over, give over
thy midnight mischief.

A chance encounter might be engineered.

A pilgrimage to see the Templars' mark
where Derwentwater's brother, of the Prieuré,
may pensively have placed his fingers.

You could share that.

A sound like rain across the dry church roof,
or one short cry from empty shrubbery,
might get you talking in that haunted place.

XXI

This is your summer, and the oak tree
grips its leaves about my face.

The last Leveller that was shot to death:
a face of leaves
that stares back smiling at your own.

It took five tons of oak to smelt one ton
of iron, a skelp of land to feed one sheep.

For you, we ranting Angels might have turned
oak roots in the wards of earth
to unlock England for her cheated yeomanry.

The very shadow frighted you
and shook your kingdome.

Rout out the titled man in every hollow,
unfurling park land, dunning for his rents!

The substantiality of levelling is comming.

XXII

Sinne and transgression is finisht,
a meere riddle, that they
with all their humane learning cannot reade.

North Tyne, untarnished by the moon, I see
still flows stealthily by Houxty. A shield
of pasture there may yet contain
the like of that heraldic bull
whose glimmering stillness strengthened me, the night
we wove our stratagem within the wood.

Alan, that was my lost bride Helen's brother,
my father, busy as a gnat,
poor drunken Marjorie: their divers ends
I cannot know. Together with myself,
whose death you must be privy to,
this was our one flesh dwindled to its remnant.

Some beer, some scraps of bread and meat, a sword,
two knives, and one great pistol
my father brandished like the cuddy's jawbone
Samson hefted, owning neither shot nor powder:
these, with my silver whistle and a Bible,
comprised our final commonwealth.

Thou and thy Family are fed,
as the young ravens strangely.

XXIII

Then, since we mortal lovers are,
ask not how long our love will last;
but while it does, let us take care
each minute be with pleasure passed.

Her boots and anorak
are in the kitchen with a residue
of spaghetti carbonara, cheese and apples,
and Côtes du Roussillon Villages.

She's heard of Rennes le Château and the Prieuré,
and shares your view
across Greenrigg to Derwentwater's stone
and light withdrawing.

I see that she herself removes,
after her dungarees and Oxfam jumper,
surprisingly upmarket underwear
and helps you slip into the grateful place
last occupied by Dr Pordage.

Did Daphnis and his nymph, or Danaë
beneath her shower of gold enjoy
such raptures in Arcadia?

XXIV

Twigs drawn in half-dark from my father's fist
decide our parts: Alan shall play
the stout cajoling pedlar, I, with fierce
and silent eloquence, his burden.

We have, of rope and canvas taken
by stealth from Marjorie's chandler's yard,
sufficiency, though it be foul.

Lee Hall is Troy, its garrison
a housemaid and a gardener
who wags a blunderbuss named Copenhagen.

Deliver, deliver,
my money that thou hast to rogues,
whores and cut-purses, who are flesh of thy flesh,
or els by my selfe, saith the Lord,
I will torment thee day and night.

Colonel Ridley's heathen treasure
will buy us passage to America
and land for freeborn Angels to rejoice in.

An unkind wind
strews silver on the river's velvet
counter like a money lender.

XXV

Give over thy base and stinking formall grace
before and after meat, give over
thy nasty, stinking family duties,
thy Gospell Ordinances;
for under them lies snarling, snapping,
biting, covetousnesse, evill surmising,
envy, malice, and horrid hypocrisie.

Give over, or if nothing els will do it,
I'l make thy child, in whom thy soul delighted,
lie with a whore before thine eyes.

By that base thing, that plaguy holinesse
and righteousnesse of thine shall be confounded,
and thou plagued back, damned and rammed
into thy mother's womb that is Eternity.

Then thou shall see no evill furthermore
but rather one huge beauty,
but first lose righteousness and holinesse
and every crum of thy Religion.

XXVI

Your duck-down duvet jerks and slides.

Now I can address you both. Outside,
thin snow sheets a whinstone bed.

Is my borrowed voice too faint? Too loud?

I fear I am no better hand
at haunting than at levelling:
beneath my slab, a bone-cache
tangled in the yew tree's roots,
I wait for recognition and for naming
while witnessing my own conception.

Ther's my riddle.

My hinny in her poor bunched shroud,
thrown from the lathered back of Heatherbell,
had the swan-begotten queen for namesake,
and yet still waits for burial
unless a mine or hag received her.

I know that beasts more easily return,
their souls more apt,
as Heatherbell the roan came back
to haunt The Orchard for the apple
your new love gave her.

Feare thou not,
creep forth a little in this mystery.

XXVII

Time rattles in the ewe's throat
and time would faile if I would tell you all.

I saw diversity, variety, distinction
and as clearly saw
all folded into Unity,
and that has been my song since then.

The dead do not know who they are
until they are remembered.

XXVIII

She steps towards me in the early morning.

A lantern flares, and Copenhagen utters
the word that lifts me
above the stink of my own blood.

My cloth womb splits.

In Houxty wood,
mist turns to smallest rain to make
visible a shift of air
that tilts the faces of the leaves.

She kneels, unwary
as she quickens, finding pipe-ash lichen,
oyster lichen, tiny rubies
delightful on my narrow stone.

It was thus resembled,
as if a great brush dipt in whiting
should sweep a picture off a wall.

The voice you hear has made itself your child.

from NOCTUA

THE BORDER

To stop and gaze here is to worship
and then, by worshipping, to close the gap
that falls between us and the pulse of things.

This is the veritable border.

When I was young they called the place a book
that presses us between its pages.

Not everyone is happy here.

Some are fearful of our agile language
that crouches just beyond their understanding:
the concert of our streams and woods,
our singing flowers.

Our staple product now is marvels:
the man, for instance, up the valley,
who grows new clothes upon himself in summer
with something itchy in the lining
that makes him shrug them off each winter.

FAIRYTALE

The children dream a foray, and their bodies
follow on their hands and knees
out from the forest, under barbed wire fences.

The wind among the trees is scolding.

A company of white geese by the stream,
down where the lane goes through a farmyard
overhung and dark with oaks,
are moonlit so that they resemble
excisions from an older, radiant world.

These are dream geese, docile, and too beautiful
to raise their wings in clamour, or to scatter.

Breath keeps pace as bare soles, gladdening
to soft damp earth and smell of prey,
accelerate a measured run,
and this is good, and this is human nature.

Wolf-girls, wolf-boys, spread your arms
find balance, vocalise your hunger.

Each night the geese are there again, but stronger.

THE OPERATION

What are, in daylight, as I told you,
pleasant things to every sense,
change shape at night when I am wakeful.

You've read the chillers that describe
the cold and bony arm around the shoulders
when no one's there, or an insistant
whisperer as dawn approaches.

Fooleries like that would make me chuckle.

My sign tonight shall be the hawk,
twenty feet above the heather,
that drew my eye and, falling, disappeared.

It seems to me that I must close
on fear and nourishment the same way, quickly.

I liked the sunshine through your window,
your cared-for room, its glow and dapple,
the pictures on your wall, your garlic crusher,
the table, scrubbed-up for the operation.

What distances there are between these facts
and what is inward, what they most resemble,
will vanish in the swiftness of my hunger.

THE TASK

Those outbuildings store what has been
abandoned now for fifty years,
where something whimpers, and the floor is slippy.

The moon will rise, and she can plainly
make out roofs against the stars,
as flimsy as a nursery prayer, and not
to be relied on in the coming weather.

Last night she found a broken china saucer.

The sort of light is growing that halts rivers,
turns back the wheel of sky, and brings
trees downhill, like marching phantoms.

Such light is perfect, and the task is simple.

She is revisiting a smile, the one
her mother used instead of kindness,
each time she comes here, choosing things
with which to build the framework of her anger.

INUYUCOY

At night, there is a kind of creature here
that has an eye of light, a radiance
you would not think could grace the world.

Wait, and it will enter from the garden,
its plumage swishing, on all fours,
and full of love and information.

This beast does not endure abuse or capture,
because it baffles all designs
by sudden darkness, or by sudden dazzle.

When love and news have been acknowledged,
you'll see it flop asleep upon the carpet,
its splendour veiled, like furniture
you never meant to have in your possession.

THE PEAR TREE

Yes, a scarecrow has been waiting for me
where the path curves, and a deep stone seat
crumbles under moss and ivy.

He wears tatters, and my favourite hat
to crown a head whose only face is bone.

See how he bends to sit, though he is fleshless,
requiring neither rest nor comfort.

The way he hugs his shakes reminds me
of flame, but dark, a flicker that's inimical
to warmth, or light, or celebration.

His thoughts are worms and crimson centipedes.

Cheer up, he'll make sure I don't linger,
but press right on towards the point
at which all paths converge, the central clearing
the pear tree stands in that we climbed as children
with all the joy least easy to remember.

CHEZ GAVIN

Fear for his head, perhaps, makes him forget
that every winter is a threshold.

Meanwhile, because it is his turn to wound me,
I ought to warn him not to be surprised
to find my blood is green, or ochre maybe,
and has the detritus of woodland in it:
perhaps the droppings of a stoat, a tangled spider,
types of moss, or little twigs.

I won't though, since he wants to scoff
and trawl for facts in pools of mystery.

Firelight is noted for that quality,
when shining upwards on a face,
of simulating rage or pain, and downwards
across a hearthrug, rivulets
of ordinary human blood.

It's late, and past the time he should beseech
confide the fight to me, let it be mine!

We've had his facts in foison, and full dishes:
perhaps I should direct him to the axe.

WOODSMOKE

after Piero di Cosimo

Whoever stands as you do at this window,
looking out from where you are exactly,
will see the things that you see start to happen.

Sky-shapes that hang between the trees
catch light like dawn, but dawn too early
to wake the pigeons or the calling crane.

The forest kindles, filling up with voices
that sing in tune with your attention.

Then something like the sunrise comes, and men
disguised as animals run out towards you
and fall, but after falling rise
as animals like you, disguised as men.

THE LITTLE FLAME

Here is the place, and where they kept
his childhood in a locked room off the kitchen.

You still require a chair to reach
the key upon its hook above the dresser.

This window is the one at which he saw
the little flame that crept down from the woods
above the house, the night before
they stopped believing what he had to tell them.

Nothing is reliable or modern,
but sunset has arrived to tint the fleeces
of flocks that do not fear the wolf or lion,
and life here will be good with decent plumbing,
an Aga, and sufficient time
to warm the world you're ready to imagine.

THE PUNT *NIXIE*

The river can be unrelenting
when no one says: let's get back home
and not tie up here and begin to whisper
so close against the ear of sunset
with ground mist rising in the nearer fields.

You classify experience by colour,
and what you tell me in your greyest voice
concerns grey streams, grey swimmers in them,
and how your secret life is grey,
shot through with pain like red light on the water.

All this is difficult to disentangle
in twilight, under willow branches.

THE FOSSIL

She knows that it is risky, nowadays,
woken by chance and in the dark,
not to keep herself in focus.

Last night she had been slithering
back into the quarry basin,
the thick green water and the jewelled silt.

She thinks of people and professions
there to help her, in their fashion.

She thinks of sweet, unconscious preservation
in sediment, her life a gem
of which she only knows the special virtue.

Is she a bat-like thing? A hippogriff?

The self she had not thought she could remember
has left a path to be completed.

She sees again, in landscape squeezed of light,
her early footprints, each claw perfect,
blurring, then in turn unblurring,
in thin dust drifting at the quarry's rim.

UNCLE GEORGE AND THE SNOW BUNTING

Finches among hawthorn berries,
and then the quickness of a yellowhammer,
refresh him, and the wren that flies
unerringly within the hedge
next to the lane below the rectory.

Without a sound, meanwhile, he enters
the wood, beside the keeper's gibbet.

Along the margin of an unpaid bill
that bears a butcher's thumbprint, like a seal,
he lists the leaf-like scraps of moles and squirrels,
weasels, stoats, a whiff of rotting,
black feathers and the beaks of crows,
a magpie with its tail in tatters,
the speckled breasts of sparrowhawks and kestrels,
their voided eyes, two tawny owls
revolving as a slight wind moves.

Tirrip, chiss-ick, chiss-ick, tee-ewe.

Inside his hat there is a winter bird
he went in search of once, that flutters
through snowflakes like a butterfly
in places hard to climb to and austere,
but pretty in those fading sketches
he brought back from his student holiday.

Lead, kindly Light, amid the encircling gloom,
    Lead thou me on;
The night is dark, and I am far from home;
    Lead thou me on.

It's hard to have much patience with a ghost
that shrivels to such earnestness:
his wretched socks, his narrow boots, the rain
his sombre clothes soak up, the pain
of fast-receding faith, all these remain
Victorian, as solemnly perverse
as long repining for a love unspoken.

And yet what strength it had, that piety
with which chums down from varsity
sang Newman to the frosty air, and, later,
how strong the hope that brings him seeking
those linked arms as he falls through time, and laughter.

·

THE DAMP HARMONIUM

The sea is cold, the moon is veiled,
and clouds are frantic with the coming storm.

A salt-bleached stile leads down to where
the graveyard is, and milky foam
embroiders rocks, as rising swell
attacks the shore and falls back, breaking.

Tonight a ship must surely founder.

The only craftsman on the island
has cut down every tree there was,
and now he is reduced to driftwood
to make his souvenirs and toys
and all the coffins in his workshop.

It's true that here we see the world
as if it were a long way off
until the ocean brings it closer.

The village hall is furnished as a chapel:
the minister has long departed
and yet his congregation comes
unsummoned at the hour of worship.

The storm breaks and the lamps grow dim.

See how the drowned have filled the doorway,
incandescent in their youth and beauty,
and how the damp harmonium is gleeful.

Please stand and join us as we raise our voices
to sing the island's only hymn.

THE PIGEON LOFT

No doubt you will have heard of his remark
that firelight on a darkened window
resembled all that seemed to stand
between him and the fecund, various world
from out of which his powers came.

He was adept at obfuscation.

He also may have said that music flies
into the ears on small black wings:
but attribution there is shaky.

Somehow, during his sojourn in Prague,
he found material for those delusions
for which his short career is now remembered.

We are unlikely to discover,
behind the smoke-clouds and dark instruments,
where exactly research led him,
or what he let loose in the pigeon loft.

He earned a bonfire for himself, that's clear
if you examine the aghast expression
he wears in that last woodcut, or the knock-
kneed verses of his *True Confeſſion*.

THE SISTERS

Broad steps with parapets ascend
from waste ground where the slicks reflect
streetlights near the underpass.

Leaping arches and emblazoned glass
confront the backs of factories.

A dwarf is bowing in embroidered flounces.

He leads us through impossible apartments:
one houses minerals, another pictures,
and farther on there's china, bronzes.

Here is the Cedar Boudoir, where the sisters
approached delirium, with even
their most minute and common parts
hand-crafted into ornament.

Outside, the buses have stopped running.

A dog I do not like trots with me,
his collar richly stitched with emblems
I am unwilling to bend down to see.

SQUIFFY

This trek has been like never learning,
with every step the same mistake,
and something vital left behind
among the trees, down where the fever swarms
vibrate beneath the heavy leaves.

What he's been looking for is there, abruptly,
and then the mountain elbows out the view.

Yes, there it is again, the shimmering house,
with its verandah in a wedge of dark,
tethered to its track out from the bush.

There is no sign of cooking-smoke, or cattle,
no dog is barking in the stable-yard.

The air is still, the mid-day light impartial.

It's time for him to start the long descent
towards the camp-bed in the shade, the gramophone.

It's strange how one idea sticks in his head.

It's nothing, really, only a daftness:
like the chap who once, back home, got squiffy
and fought a goblin on the vicar's lawn.

BREATHE CAREFULLY

In your attic there could be a shrouded globe,
some tinsel, flashbulbs, and a picture book.

If not, some bobbins and a rocking horse,
or, better still, an old piano stool,
a dusty window, and a dying moth:
it doesn't matter, work with what you find,
so long as you have all you need for stitching.

When you see the man-shape and its shadow,
look right through them, make the voice of thunder.

The job, of course, must not remain too solid.

Peel off one dimension, make it flat
enough to slide the whole thing sideways
into the future of your certain person,
precisely when he turns away abruptly,
dismissing you, and is not mindful
of your importance, his fragility.

If this seems difficult, go back
and practise basic wrapping and unfolding.

Nothing is achieved without expenditure:
before you start, try emptying your purse
into an unfamiliar ditch or culvert
while snow falls, and the beggars are in shelter.

Breathe carefully, a little at a time,
unhook the phone, and bolt your door.

THE SINGERS

The place has contrasts of a kind:
damp cobblestones and fog up in the heights,
blown sand below among deserted wharves,
salt-flats, and hulks with tilting spars.

Mama assaults embroidery.

Her blue-eyed girls address their music
among the ghosts of pioneers.

How shall the singers meet the song?

On patient feet, the longed-for invitations
take both their lifetimes to arrive.

Meanwhile, their great-grand-neice flies in
to bathe her jet-lag, change, and carry
her first aperitif onto the terrace
to catch the sunset on the hulkless sea.

The barman sulks like her psychiatrist.

Aloft, two gulls with human eyes behold
her stab her handbag for a cigarette,
then perch themselves upon the balustrade
to contemplate her slenderness of wrist.

THE INTERVENTION

Now that we have made the aperture
between the pillow and the head, we can
quite easily insert a panorama.

Tonight I think we'll use the estuary
together with a dreamy landscape,
reflecting back the setting sun.

It is traditional, but most effective.

The patient will remember vast
receding distances, and yet
they are of course minute from our perspective.

Nightmares that congregate to kiss
their own reflections as they stoop to drink
present the only problem with this option.

We must allow time for their games
of hide-and-seek and writhing hurly-burly,
before they vanish from the shallows
to merge with stillness and the rosy light.

At this point do not dilly-dally.

If we are slow to make the intervention,
then we may lose the patient at the instant
that sunset starts to leave the water
in darkness to become the river
that is too wide and deep for us to cross.

THE LEVEL ISLAND

The rich confusions he achieved
by patient effort and self-sacrifice
have been disposed of, with his few successes.

How right he is to set out early,
this afternoon of doubtful weather,
before full onset of the crepuscule.

He is surprised that no one comes
to see him off along the road,
or ask him to postpone his journey.

Sharp slants of green cut through the gloom.

He knows the slope towards the lough,
the forest, and the level island
he dreamed of once, with heather burning.

Each step he takes contributes more to silence,
unburdened by the luggage of his limbs.

He hears the worms in thawing soil
make progress, and a hawthorn bush
whisper about breaking buds.

At last his talents will be used.

Warm air from distances arrives
like understanding, and his silly face
begins to quiver and to itch with leaves.

JIGGER NODS

Warner, whose immortal pen
praised every honest Englishman
that strives to set old Albion free
from giants of adversity,
founded our school and built our rule
in good Queen Bess's reign.

The Founder's Anthem

We think no greater blisse than such
to be as be we would,
when blessèd none but such as be
the same as be they should.

William Warner, *Albion's England*

I

Is it still visible, the bright
imaginary green,
within this future we are moving to?

Jigger sees it, all a dazzle,
beyond the monkeypuzzle tree.

II

Wind, time, and sun reel shadows back
to flicker over market stalls
towards the coke-works and the shunting yard,
a transport café lodged beneath an arch,
and hinterland where sooty hills are dozing.

There, in that town, are the fleet of foot,
the armoured and the many-headed.

Stables brim and reek, a thousand
inky essays wait for marking,
and amazons rebuff him, one by one,
except Hippolytë, who leaves
her girdle on the field of battle.

Ex pede Herculem!

The world is worse than it was then,
thinks Jigger, with a crooked troupe
of immigrants and nancy-boys
exploiting Albion, and grinding down
the spirit of her Englishmen.

III

For many years he livèd thus,
stipended so to live,
and shepherd-like to teach a flock
himself did wholly give . . .

Put your feet up, Hercules.

An armchair, whisky, and a smoke,
improve the taste of goading boys
towards a rumour of applause
that's fainter as the years go on
and banish thoughts of Iphicles,
the one your mother loved the best,
who was her husband's only son.

No need to struggle with the tall sash now.

Outside the eighteen darkening panes
lies all the sorrow of the Masters' Garden,
where beehives and exotic trees
stand spectrally in mist that hides
the empty playing-fields, and then
the valley's steeper banks, its flow.

IV

It's safer to be drunk than think.

What was that certainty, the day
he crumpled, as his wife confessed
the focus of her restlessness,
then beat a slithery retreat
in hobnails and a waterproof,
that he had somehow glimpsed himself,
androgynous and beckoning,
a long way off across a planted field?

Thought salvaged him, and it was merely
a scarecrow in a cotton dress.

V

Boys barge from fart-filled rooms, and men
on tiptoe from the common-room
leave Jigger to his lonely ease
as something frets the outside dark
and taps the glass as if to enter.

O zonam perdidit!

Somewhere today he lost the key
that swung in retributive arcs
inside the long sleeve of his chalky gown.

His Latin tags are fatuous.

Ozone is what he needs, not drink,
perchance a holiday, meanwhile
his spectacles are gone, his books, his pen
that cut with scarlet *ynke*:
schoolmastering oppresses only
the shadows of its silly boys.

VI

Brute suppressed the Albinests,
huge giants, fierce and strong,
and of this isle, un-Scotted yet,
he empire had ere long . . .

When Jigger nods and dreams the end
of titan Albion and all
his upstart swarthy Albinests,

he sees true Albion, the land, released,
eponymous, that Trojan Brute
and all fair-skinned, fair-minded Brutons
may tramp in peace their native hills.

Such views were rife when he attended
the University of Troy Novant.

VII

Recall that morning, spiked with pot-pourri,
when sunlight and suburban air
asked simply that he knuckle down
to make sense of that how-do-you-do
of lipstick messages, the rage
of underwear Hippolytë
took off with her and twice the man
that he was then, black-skinned and ardent,
borne up on U.S. Air Force wings.

For as the Smith with hammers beats
his forgèd metal, so
he dubs his club about their pates
and fleas them in a row . . .

Those other mornings were more happy,
when, hopping to avoid the plop,
he swished a stick, bold *claviger*,
to shoo the big cat on the farmyard wall,
while Deianira, Iole, and Hebe,
led the herd, with flailing tails,
down towards the dangerous pasture
that held the river and the anglers' hut,
to leave him swinging on the gate, an imp
in wellingtons, no longer Henry
but one the vicar, in his jovial way,
would call his infant Hercules.

VIII

Her upper parts had humaine forme,
her nether Serpentine,
the whole was monstrous, yet her wit
more monstrous, was most fine . . .

A spring within the armchair twangs.

It seems the scarecrow has begun
to add to beckoning a voice
that undermines his snug, well-worn regret
that he is old and drunk already
and never was an Oxford man.

IX

Now the door is not quite shut.

A need is scratching to come in, an itch
for more than that corrosive fable
of blowing roadside oaks and elms
and gates in hedgerows that reveal
those gleaming meadows, snowy orchards,
and parks in which ancestral piles
stand, among great-hearted timber,
for all that Dornford Yates and Jigger
think Englishness amounts to in the end.

Here comes a question and a wounding
that wakes him to confront the dark.

Eheu fugaces . . . labuntur anni!

Outside, each fallen leaf records
the grieving of the arboretum.

X

Alas that from the lab stinks rise.

Boy-haunted passages are glooming fast:
no time to ogle photographs
of First XIs, First XVs,
or keep an eye on changing rooms.

Aut insanit homo aut versus facit!

Yes, Sir, we know that you eschewed
perverse insanitary deeds.

XI

Just like the spook in Betton Wood,
or Alfred's child, the scarecrow speaks
and has no language but a cry
that makes her grinning topknot tremble
above the snake-shreds of her frock.

The landscape of his pain still holds
the flutter of her hesitation
positioned where a cloud adjusts
and readjusts, as in a loop,
the envelope of light in which
she seems unable to complete
the half-turn she has almost made.

Obscurum per obscurius!

It seems she calculates the cost
of entry to a human heart,
and, scenting lack of will, resolves
to try her skill at bilocation.

Her cut-throat grin becomes a gap
between the inner and the outer dark
through which thin mischief starts to seep.

XII

The black man, grinning as he mounts a wing
to reach the cockpit of his plane,
has bleached to buff before he falls
off the locker, by the bed
in which Hippolytë is doped asleep,
and shatters glass and no one sees
the cleaner bin him, fearing censure.

GOODBYE TO DR IPHICLES

A photo from the evening paper
is also quickly binned, compressed
to pellet-form and lobbed by Jigger.

It shows the town's most liked GP
beside his wife and smiling colleagues,
multiracial, un-class-conscious,
for *au-revoirs* before he flies
to serve in long-postponed retirement
with Médecins Sans Frontières.

XIII

The hives are sleeping, and no honey bees
could replicate what he can hear
outside the window, in the monkeypuzzle.

It is a sibilance that scarecrows find
torments the kind of men who look
at women as into a mirror
to see the face of what they loathe.

It's not just women Jigger trusts
to make him squirm, but all their flock
of nancy-boys and fancy-men,
and jungle-monkeys on the make,
and Celtic whingers with their paws
about the throat of Albion.

To lacke life lost in chalke and ynke:
an hell, an hell, an hell . . .

A time arrives when what he thinks
is coiled so tight about his chest
that fear and rage unreconciled
grow hot enough to scorch his vest.

The lilac waits beside the oak.

More subtle than the ghosts of ghosts
are all the causes in their ancient files
of what he is, and must now lose.

XIV

Does he still hope for company?

Then fill an afternoon with summer heat,
the breathy rub of thirty boys,
the shipboard creak of desks, the creep
of Platignum and Osmiroid.

Is there a danger to the perfect grass?

Jerk up the window, out with him and under,
arms and legs a movie flicker,
to kite his black and tattered sleeves
towards the shimmering cricket square
where, in the haze, dark limbs and creamy
entwine in ecstasy unnoticed
by men who mow, and mark the creases.

How fair she was, and who she was,
she bore for him the bell
that knew although he clownish is
the place where beauty dwells . . .

This moment holds the hours, and years.

Wake up the organ with the Founder's Anthem,
let sunlight play on beeswaxed floors
and trophies, mustered in a silver dazzle
as if for battle, on a field of flowers.

Have sashes squeak, and schoolboy faces
cling like sediment to sills and sides
of lofty windows, eighteen-paned,
to see a burnished car deposit,
to comic bugles of the Corps, and birdsong
never heard so clearly since,
a royal duchess, polka-dotted,
with long silk gloves whose fingers reach
down forty years to squeeze his fingers.

Non nisi malis terrori!

Beneath her condescending smile,
thin sticks are what her dress hangs on.

XV

The sooty hills have shuffled off
their weight of visibility:
allotments where the town thins out
are compartmentalising dusk.

As quick as breath, let's be aboard
the train home through a fading day.

All night, cold lights of combines turn
to shave straight edges of the crop
then turn again: hauled in their wake,
jolting balers pack the hay.

XVI

Whose father's room, whose father's bed,
is where this broken breathing is?

Bis pueri senes!

This lad should not be here at all
alone at this late early time,
the stillest of a summer night,
when childhood ends with harvest baled
and scattered in the stubble fields.

He should not stand too near this window
or dare to breathe such altered air.

Fear and freedom are his chums,
clasp-knife-wielding, boy-scout-belted,
with bread and jam in greaseproof paper,
to track adventure to its lair
in full sun of the holidays,

out by the pungent path next to the lilac
and the wide trunk of the climbing oak,
in which, among the highest branches,
his tattered kite is bravely flapping:
heraldic, irretrievable.

The bedside tick, the bedside tock,
is louder when the breathing stops.

XVII

*I'll leave here when that monkeypuzzle
puts out one bloody English rose.*

The worse for booze, a breathless grip
comes back as if his chest belonged
to him no longer, but a man
who dies each night, or else the son
he might have been, an Iphicles
whose decent, hopeful heart expands.

*The best of bees do beare, beside
sweet honey, smarting stings,
and time doth not need any baite
that unto sorrow brings . . .*

Not even when the lawyer finds
a legacy for Iphicles
and none for him, not even then
is Jigger sent to make his claim
upon the doorstep of the vicarage,
before the tall door in the rain,
on one who keeps his mother mum
and offers nothing but her blame.

XVIII

Silence strikes its longest note.

Time dawdles where the scarecrow flickers,
as if projected through an inner lens
onto his wall of snug regrets,
and mocks and frocks him like a sailor's floozy,
while Christmas holidays repeat, and summers
go by with minor maintenance:
the school asleep through tinker shuffles
late every morning of the mops and pails.

More bloody darkies every term.

What wakes the hives among the leaves
that scab the lawn like dead skin dropping?

Again the pain recedes, and whisky
dilates his throat the more to croak
a mockery of banter,
not laughable, an obstacle to laughter.

The loop breaks and the scarecrow moves.

XIX

The whole was monstrous, yet her wit,
more monstrous, was most fine,
and fed on fear and spite she thus
confounded all she found,
propounding questions, and a word
unanswered was a wounde . . .

Heartbeats that activate the air
like tiny eddies of departure
disturb the room and silence causes
their echoes, barely short of stillness,
to wax inquisitorial.

How noiselessly the tall sash rises.

She's found your bolt-hole, Henry Jigger,
master of the sleepy arts
of armchair and tobacco jar,
by way of ramblers' paths and roads
turned serpentine, and boy-scuffed rooms,
and labs and halls and corridors,
and trees and hives where mist conceals
what slithers in the Masters' Garden.

XX

If only once, he should have skipped
behind the herd into the sun
that tipped their horns with gold, and turned,
as Warner sings, a crab, perhaps,
or tuned a round to test the morning
as far as to the farthest pasture,
contemptuous of his comeuppance.

Dum vivimus, vivamus!

Likewise, the necessary grit
to be a comrade to a restless wife
and fund a family, and find
it, if not grateful, well-disposed,
might now have helped him face the dark
and dust that settles all he chose.

They sweetly surfeiting in joy
and silent for a space,
whenas the ecstacy had end
did tenderly embrace.

An hell then, speechless Vivimus?

Its topknot level with his open window
in murk that thickens as he peers
to see what something outside is,
the araucaria extends its fingers
to shelter nothing, and to shed no leaves.

XXI

Alas, the fleeting years, alas
the nursing home that drearily
accommodates Hippolytë
and swindles Dr Iphicles.

She and her twice-the-man, now unremembered,
share their moment with the zephyr
that makes the scarecrow beckon, and caresses
the tassel on the mortarboard
of Jigger by the the royal car,
the day he hears the organ grumble
in concert with the bugles and the birds.

Hebe, Iole, and Deianira,
for the last time in that selfsame moment
re-enter the forbidden pasture.

That moment, neither tick nor tock,
is at the window when poor Jigger
falls as if he falls for ever
from childhood into altered air.

Necessitas non habet legem!

For leglessness, a final dram
is once again what we require.

XXII

He is too pusillanimous
upon this other windowsill
to trust the voice that calls him out
to play the man and earn his wings
above the fives court and the Bursar's house,
the shut pavilion and the stud-pocked fields.

But Hercules is brave and young
among the footholds of the oak
whose branches close and then fall back
before his blows, bold *claviger*,
until his black kite lifts away
its academical and chalky tatters,
and clambers up the playful sky.

XXIII

It's Jigger's turn to spook the eye:
his bee-swarm of the heart becomes
a palanquin that bears him up
like Brutus into Albion
above the tree-tops of the Masters' Garden
triumphally, then lets him drop.

The hives vibrate.

A tattered tongue uncoils and spits
while polka-dots of dapples fall
in strange light where a shive of summer
warms the duchess, in the arboretum,
her snake-shreds sloughed and wearing daisies
entangled in her pubic hair,
for waggle-dancing, and the splits.

So who can equal Hercules
by whom the monster fell
who, burning up her ugly shape,
did passe her soule to hell?

Tonight Her Royal Highness finds
herself the lithe embodiment
of lewd and ludicrous delight, wherefrom
the voice proceeds that soothes the bees.

XXIV

Contraries be the elements,
at strife contraries fall,
yeat Sea, the Earth, the Aier, them both,
the skie be-cleaps them all . . .

Inside the café, as the trains go over,
a greasy banner of St George stirs gently
above the bone-pale heads of Brutons.

On hinterland where hills are dozing,
and neighbourhoods where black and white
share terraces beside the tracks,
a mosque, a synagogue, and many churches,
on market stalls of jeans and saris,
and softly on the flat-roofed day-room
in which, upon a high-seat chair,
Hippolytë is sitting, dreaming,
autumn dampness turns to drizzle.

Meanwhile, an odd, unlovely rose,
blood-scumbled, will be stretchered down
and pouched among the fallen leaves.

Recreant wretch, he Albion loved
and wished her to be free,
that causèd him to suffer on
a cruel outlandish tree . . .

Across the lawn, three policewomen,
Iole, Deianira, Hebe,
as if in mourning, gather clothes,
a hearing-aid and shoes, a watch-chain,
in line with a trajectory
a jump for England might have barely managed
from window-sill to monkeypuzzle.

Your native rain, O Hercules, dissolves
the Hydra's venom in the blood
and cools your overheated vest.

XXV

Nor meete it were, in Justice or
in nature, things of nought
shall equal that unbounded Power
that All of Nothing wrought.

That be not Two or divers Gods
is also prompt by this,
and vanitie is Period
of everie thing that is.

Of One all Multiplicities,
Formes, Harmonies, (what not?)
be, howsoere they seeme confused,
producèd and begot.

Of whichsoere all creatures be
compounded formally,
so then of contrarieties
is Uniformitie.

To one Sea flow all Fluds, one Sunne
inlighteneth every Light,
of all celestiall Movings is
one Mover, artists write.

Trunke, barke, boughs, leaves, and blossomes, none
like others hath a Tree,
yet but one Roote, whence all, which but
one Author's act can bee.

XXVI

Somewhere a bell, elsewhere a morning
choir is on its feet and singing:

Behold a teacher, with the Sun
he doth his flocke engage
and all the day with ynke and chalk
he merry warre can wage,
and with the Sun doth fold again,
then jogging home betime,
he turns a crab, or tunes a round,
or sings some merry rhyme . . .

Thus Warner's verse, the driest work
entrusted yet to pen and *ynke*,
floats down like cobweb scraps to settle
as dust upon an empty chair
from which a man in pain and drink
has clambered into air and gone
beyond the tall sash, eighteen-paned,
to friendly distances where hills,
no longer sooty, wake to welcome,
conjubilant, the dauntless boots
and anoraks of Albion.

XXVII

The organ heaves its direst rumble
while coughing and snot-noises die.

The choir attacks *Jerusalem*,
then struggles up a notch to raise
Warner whose immortal pen
as high as maybe, where poor Jigger,
on thermals of hyperbole
has reached the bright imaginary green
and found at last within the dazzle
his shape and size of place exactly.

XXVIII

Voices disperse, and choristers
resume their lives without rehearsal.

Above their heads, the organist
deserts his nest and switches off
the light that lit the keys and stops.

Desks slam like starting-guns: a plangent fart
drives on the day like any other.

XXIX

Half-mast, a brighter red cross shifts
as mist thins in the Masters' Garden
and burns to snake-trails on the playing fields.

Whenas the ecstacy has end, the skies
within this future we are making
unclasp the ground while Albion
hugs yet more closely what her myths disguise.

XXX

The sweet o' the year is rising up
so dewy and so odorous
from out of England's snowy orchards,
to scent the isle, all lands excelling,
where Jigger has inherited
the long dream of her heights and woods,
the freedom of her unmapped meadows.

Fuimus Troes!

Fag-ash and whisky glass survive
a dwindling moment as he slips
the minds of feckless sons of Brutus.

Their clownish shapes a coined show,
the poore schoolmasters weep,
schoolmasters weep and they are woe,
and then do silence keep.

Yet soldier on, thou frumious Trojans,
turn blackboards into cliffs of chalk
in those true-blue academies
from which no Englishman retires, wherein
no women and no scarecrows dwell,
and skirmish joyfully with silly boys
like Blake, and Shakespeare, and Purcell.

APOKATASTESIS

APOKATASTESIS

Her three cats by the hallstand leapt
in three directions when they heard my voice.

She pointed to the rain-cleansed garden
outside the window, and her roses
with moisture clinging, and refracted light.

I resolutely broached our current topic:
apokatastesis, the restitution
in all creation of its lost perfection.

Think kindly, Reader, and forgive
my subsequent discourtesy.

For then I noticed she'd retouched,
in villainous vermilion,
the lovely nostrils of my rocking-horse.

My wisdom is an extinct bird
that flaps its wings and scatters dust.

Her innocence is like a beast
that must be rapped upon the snout, like pity.

OGRESS

You think I only cook, and clean, and launder?

I used to yoke the oxen, and the elephant,
to pull his wheelchair to the height
through veils of rain, so he could watch
the playful mountains throwing rocks
until the valleys shook their sides
and all the beasts ran from the woods.

He has been known to curdle frost
on winter mornings with a look, and yet
that spectacle could sometimes make him smile.

Your little world would no doubt condescend
to laugh at this, and at our oddity –
his size, my warty skin and single eye –
but no one comes here now, and laughter,
so unbecoming in the well-brought-up,
is never heard in these grey vastnesses.

He should have recognised his own good luck.

I did not need him to inform me
how well I suit my situation
by virtue of monstrosity,
when I considered it a privilege
to serve him while I could, unstintingly.

His punishment is now to drag his body
up marble stairs alone, night after night,
each riser higher than the last, each step
with what he owes me carved into the tread.

EQUESTRIENNE

His readers always said he loved
a circus girl, and left her in the lurch,
when he was young and fancy-free,
because he wrote as if he knew
exactly how it feels to ride
with one leg raised and balanced at the gallop
while pregnant by a novelist.

The man himself is reticent, but claims
she started as an image on a poster
he noticed peeling off a wall
while motoring in France between the wars.

It's known as cognitive fluidity.

We have a witness, though, quite elderly,
a bare-back rider once herself, it seems,
who says that she can take us to the graves
not only of the girl, but of the pony.

LISTENING-DUTY

Last night she told me all about the house
that dances: its façades
turquoise and lime, sometimes magenta,
changing colour as it bobs and twirls
away from England and its damp, grey light.

You can imagine her, I'm sure,
small and exotic in the well
of that high room above the bomb-sites
and moonlit porticoes:
Belgravia, with black-out paint
still covering the windows on the stairs.

Her background-story doesn't gel,
and yet I can detect a pattern
that always pulls us in the same direction.

Tonight, before I go off listening-duty,
the check-points and the customs-sheds
of Europe will be up and dancing,
and policemen, in their heavy boots.

QUICK MOVERS

The sea encroaches on the coast, and now
an absence left by some quick mover
among the branches of the sycamore
arrives upon the instant that you think
you see at last what counts and what to live for.

All longing is, you say, the wish
to be received into such absence.

The garden and the tree won't last the winter,
but here for once is impulse where it's wanted.

There is so little green left on the lawn,
bleached as it is by salt and summer light,
that rabbits sit and eat their shadows.

In boldness and simplicity, lead on.

We'll be the quickest of quick movers, leaving
buoyant absences untroubled by
the sea's rejoinder to this conversation
or all the effort that it takes to die.

THE SWEET O' THE YEAR

Wisdom will blossom in a gentleman
through slow suppression of his eagerness.

Hold back, and then, in time, proceed
towards each tantalising goal,
but make your actions slow, and incomplete.

From order down through order, links
reflect the cosmic harmony.

The sweet o' the year is yet to come.

Don't lose our vision of informing beauty
because you feel your heart is flying
to light on England's snowy orchards,
so dewy and so odorous,
and dance among her gleaming meadows.

Be patient and consult your books.

Outside, that whisper is the stream
among the sifting leaves, as if
the dead within their graves were softly breathing.

ACTE GRATUIT

My hat, discarded with its plume, resembles
a stricken bird beside us in the grasses.

My sword has been unbuckled and put by.

White clouds are hanging without motion
from nothing but a warm blue sky.

Be bold, my poppet, and, like me, resolve
upon those acts you least desire,
and unto which you have no obligation.

When I have crooked my narrow smile
and brushed your finger-tips with my moustache
in fond goodbye, your pretty head
will spin with notions and be ready
to make the mind's escape from love and duty.

Meanwhile you have been half alive, submit
your slender body to my kisses –
my *acte gratuit*, my turtle-dove, my beauty.

THE BANNER MEN

From burned-out granaries and fuel dumps
come whisperings of pain and rage,
while dogs are gnawing battle scraps
and starving as their fleas increase.

Behind this coastal plain, the sombre
hinterland wears combat dress: low walls collapse
beside the ditches they were quarried from,
and turrets shift on steeps of rubble.

Ours is a virile and a martial age.

The man who knows the routes the convoys use
has built his palace out of twisted metal,
betrayed by clues outside the entrance tunnel:
some bubblegum, a playing-card, and sputum.

His job is mending roads, for which
he hopes some government may yet reward him,
meanwhile he has hot news to barter.

He is a craftsman, and prepared to forage
for sculpture or for lettered stone,
like that with extracts from our Constitution,
or, when he can, for loot from old museums
that represents female fecundity
or gods and goddesses from cinemas.

Look how his hammer splits the face
of that fine marble Mickey Mouse,
and, as he tamps them in position,
how well the grinning fragments fit the camber.

Spare him, my brothers, while he keeps his watch.

The love of beauty dignifies his labour,
and, like we banner men, he will not grovel
or farm the land, and that is noble.

Ride on, and burn what junk he has,
yet, of our magnanimity,
allow him life for art, which is no more
or less than we enjoy, whose art is slaughter,
though we gain banners and the spoils of war.

THE THEORIST

The dark experience that makes him tick
remains unfathomed, and his phrases,
always formalised and florid,
stand like tombstones on the page, a henge
within which fog banks loom and tremble.

He is a critic to his boots, a theorist
whose layered constructs twist themselves to finger
the heart of reticence, where space
embraces emptiness, the mournful
resonance of slight and abject gesture.

Such fine distinctions tend to blur,
as every sentence that he writes confesses.

He tried to tell me once, in confidence,
what happened on the tow-path when his satchel
was snatched by big girls from the mill
who threw his school cap to the ducks
before they searched his trousers for his pencil.

THE IMP

Watch how you go, the path down there
is blocked in parts by builders' rubble,
and slippy under rotting leaves.

The house is cramped but neat, and both
the parents of the imp are solid folk,
the father clever with his hands, the mother
not knowing how to let herself be idle.

Encourage them in conversation.

They will speak proudly of its horns and tail
and rough skin, caustic to the touch.

I'll be astonished if you fail
to find the fixity of their devotion
comforting, in some ways, to the mind.

If you intend to make a close inspection,
present my compliments, and take
your gardening-gloves and overalls,
and something for the lad himself, perhaps
a horseshoe for a teething-ring.

THE ANTS

In finest health and heart, the king
is standing drinking with his bride
and close advisors when he falls,
remaining speechless to his death, whereat
a table topples and an ash-tray spills.

What we recall in anger re-occurs.

The man who is not here survives to hatch
those treacheries that deepen and intensify
the sound of loss the wind makes in the oak-wood
behind the car-park and the function-suite.

We that were disinherited inhabit
thin bodies that the years blow through.

Inch by inch, see how the careful policemen
discover, as they comb the ground,
that, like our ancient foes, the ants
are many and do bite among the mast
and pizza crusts the royal boar
we hunted here full proudly would delight in
before we slew them, as we shall again.

THE CYPHER

The air is thick up through the wood
but not oppressive in the central clearing.

You may admire what stands there all the better
for stepping forward into freshness,
and contemplate my work with no discomfort.

No Gothick flights remain, since your remarks
in your kind missive, which I have to hand,
not even the encircling verandah
I had myself contrived, for which
I nursed an artist's fondness, I confess,
together with the four tripartite arches,
the balcony, the quatrefoil and fluted friezes.

Instead, we have a domed and pillared building,
strict in design, with simple capitals
above which is *RESURGAM* and the cypher,
exactly in accordance with your wishes.

The iron door is open, as you see.

My men thought that to close it, in this weather,
except you were yourself, Sir, placed within,
might prompt the tempest, and, when all was finished,
draw down upon their heads a thunderbolt.

THE TENANT

In front there is no garden, as you see,
that's worth the name, but walls so thick
with greenery they seem like living walls.

Be kind enough to follow me.

Behind the tower itself, an acre,
laid out in the English fashion,
surveys the prospect travelled through
to reach here, that recessive vale
absorbing darkness from the evening light.

It is of course your past we're breathing:
that scent that fuses with the air.

No property we have will suit so well
a gentleman requiring, as you say,
to live exactly where he first began
to exercise his powers of fancy.

All things we think are permanent
endure a moment or a day.

The present tenant, who combines
uncommon urgency of body
with vacant looks, will be evicted
with utmost tact and in advance
of your most welcome and esteemed arrival.

MASKS

So our wormskin and paper masks still keep,
Above the rotting bones they hide,
Marks of the Plague whereof we died.

   Edith Sitwell, *Gold Coast Customs*

We have no faces since our fathers,
gurning like goblins or as grave as stones,
sold them to the Queen of Fancy
to make her belly swell with art
as you commanded when they bent their knees.

We dance in masks, like all defeated races.

The Queen of Fancy has no features either,
as you'll remember when you see her, throned
upon her doorstep in her monthly fever,
stock-still until her hand flicks out to seize
a mouse of many taught to frolic there
and squeak it until squeaking ceases.

Her lap is full of little bones.

She'll prance beside us as despair increases
and trample them, no longer mice
but pale ideograms that dart
in shadow that the noon sun gathers
about her writhing vacancy,
not caring that they wear the faces
she has forgotten that we ever owned
or smiled with in our infancy
when you unwrapped your wormskin favours
to charm us from our secret places.

THE SECRET KINGS

Grey wrists of ivy jam the doors, and skin
of still-born babies, tucked beneath the eaves,
keeps you ailing and your actions feeble.

I am the kindest of the secret kings.

My breath is die-back to the apricot
and leaf-curl to the nectarine.

The sun withdraws and female, fruiting things
grow pale with mould, while masculine
gimcrackeries, like green-house roofs or steeples,
use neither dawn nor sunset to promote
fertility by shooting smouldering glances.

I am the rattle of dissolving rain,
those crepitations of the ivy leaves
that end in sudden silences,
as if a potentate more terrible
might stalk your garden as the year advances.

THE SALLY GARDEN

Become a puppy once again
and leave your half-chewed catalogue
of wasted chances on the rug
of snug regrets and snuff the sweet
night air among the sally trees.

Gaps in the stonework of the wall, and ivy
entangled in the trellises,
seem etched by moonlight to provide
good lodgements for your teeth and paws.

I see you also now have hands and toes.

Once up, reach for the sally boughs and tug
yourself towards me while I set your feet
upon the stone head of Mnemosyne.

She's mossy, but securely placed
for you to slither down, into the fog
of what was once a paradise.

Let's see no sadness in your eyes.

I have arranged some things of yours
together in a single thought:
an awful childhood and a spade
left in the ground to rust, and scars
of earth amid the wilderness,
as if someone with half a mind
to find a good spot for a grave had dug
without conviction, or a dog
had half remembered where a bone was laid.

NARCISSUS BY AN UNKNOWN MASTER

Come up the slope into the picturesque,
you pretty creature, and enjoy
the sheep at rest about their pasture,
and geese in flight beneath the moon, disposed
according to the laws of composition.

What fails to please can be adjusted,
that dark lop-sided boskage, say,
could very quickly be improved
by silvered water or a lighted window.

I shall be waiting at the pool,
to touch the surface and make ripples snip
your face, until its smile resembles
self-satisfaction in a connoisseur,
or sly concupiscence in those
who ogle Echo, in her ivory skin,
reclining on the Golden Section
with one hand careful of her modesty.

Transformation is the price of beauty.

How cunningly my hieroglyphs
of pigment, brush-licked into place, enlist
the colours of each syllable
to blend your shape into your name, until
you lift your head in bloom to see
the nymph form *scissors* with her painted lips.

THE ANGEL

The snow is feather-like and slow descending
between the spires, and now the room
itself begins to fill with feathers
that glow and give off sounds and odours.

Put down your notebook: pass the lamp.

This is an outcome we must spare
no time or labour to suppress.

Up through the neck comes speech, the damp
core only of each vocable,
and then that diffident, sweet-natured smile
returns as if it can remember,
each time it tries to lift a wing
from off the rag rug by the study fire,
the outspread heavens, like a curtain.

Our colleagues will endorse our course of action.

This creature is too frail to bear –
pull back my shirt cuffs if you will, Professor –
our human narrowness of range and know
each hour it lives that it must die,
and meanwhile drag its feet through slush, and never
ascend in splendour into falling snow.

MISS DAPHNE

Show me those lower teeth, she said,
mouths wide, your lips well down, and sing.

We sang more like a pulse, so pure
our teacher's face put off its urging,
becoming younger in the garden,
more like an answer, a decision made.

She took her clothes off then, and danced.

That's how it was, a drowsy sound,
our lips well down, our open mouths,
while she danced all the woodland creatures
and one slim tree whose shape she has
to this day, by the summer-house.

THE MUSÉE FOLKLORIQUE

This one's our man, the Breton piper,
geared up to play outside her gate.

His shorts are goat-skin, but the beard is false.

The instrument itself is like a goat,
its leather belly gripped inside his cape.

We've got two snaps of her: one with a box
of dolls in peasant costumes, just unwrapped
from tissue paper but already damaged
quite shockingly, and, in the files
since last time she was out, we've kept
that mug-shot where she's smiling through her tears.

Our best guess was she'd borrow his disguise
and make straight for the Musée Folklorique.

Down there we heard reports of grunts and squawks
of Breton music half the night,
so that was that, we thought, case sorted,
until this morning, when the beard turned up,
with one leg only of the goat-skin trousers,
concealed behind a flower-pot
with contents we need help to analyse.

PENSÉE

Because a language is your own, the words
are stones that fit the mouth exactly.

Therefore, when you bite your tongue, be careful,
or think in silence of your broken teeth.

THE LONG PACK

The story of the long pack appears in *The Ettrick Shepherd's Tales*, and also in Elizabeth Gaskell's *Cranford*. It is well-known in the village of Bellingham, in Northumberland, where the occupant of the pack is buried in the churchyard. My long poem adds details about his earlier life, as a member of a community of ranters, to material provided by James Hogg, together with an account of some episodes in the lives of two late-twentieth-century lovers who are troubled by this desperado's restless and rather domineering spirit. The haunter's aim is to be reborn and recognised. Meanwhile he describes their experiences as well as his own, offers advice and comment, and appears sometimes in foliage, like the Green Man. The narrator also refers, perhaps unwisely, to links between members of the 1715 Jacobite uprising in Northumberland and the activities of the mysterious Prieuré de Sion, as described by Michael Baigent, Richard Leigh, and Henry Lincoln in *The Holy Blood and the Holy Grail*. The voice of Richard Last, which dominates the chorus, is adapted from the writings of the real-life ranter Abiezer Coppe. The chorus also includes quotations from Sir George Etherege, Robert Herrick, Samuel Johnson, Andrew Marvell, the anonymous author of 'Hexham Wood', and Wilfrid Gibson, whose poem 'The Unseen Rider' also mentions Heatherbell and the tragic wedding. Apart from a visit to the Coromandel coast, and to the unusual church at Hartburn, the events of 'The Long Pack' take place in the real geography of the North Tyne valley and Redesdale.

JIGGER NODS

Iphicles was the son of Amphitryon and his wife Alcmene, but his brother Hercules was the son of Zeus, who had disguised himself as Amphitryon. The relationship of Henry Jigger to his brother, the popular GP, corresponds to that between Hercules and Iphicles, though in this case Zeus has disguised himself as the vicar. As a schoolmaster, somewhere in the northern part of England in the middle of the last century, Jigger took a muddled interest in the story of the occupation of Albion by the Trojan Brutus, in which Hercules played a part. This provides no excuse for his disreputable views, moral cowardice and heavy drinking, or for his addiction to Latin tags. Quotations throughout the poem are taken or adapted from *Albion's England* by William Warner, of which C.S. Lewis wrote: 'The good things are as far divided as the suns in space.' The Latin tags may be found underlined in the section headed 'Words and Phrases in More or Less Current Use from Latin, Greek, and Modern Foreign Languages' in Jigger's copy *of Chambers's Twentieth Century Dictionary*, 1939 edition, and, for convenience, below. The exception, *Non Nisi Malis Terrori*, remains the motto of the school that employed him.

Jigger's Latin tags:

Aut insanit homo aut versus facit!
Either the man is mad or he is making verses.

Bis pueri senes!
Old men are twice boys.

Claviger
Club-bearer (or key-bearer), an epithet of Hercules.

Dum vivimus, vivamus!
While we live, let us live.

Eheu fugaces . . . labuntur anni!
Alas, the fleeting years slip away.

Ex pede Herculem!
(We recognise) Hercules by his foot.

Fuimus Troes!
We were once Trojans.

Necessitas non habet legem!
Necessity has (or knows) no law.

Obscurum per obscurius!
(Explaining) the obscure by means of the more obscure.

O zonam perdidit!
(O) he has lost his purse, he is in needy circumstances.